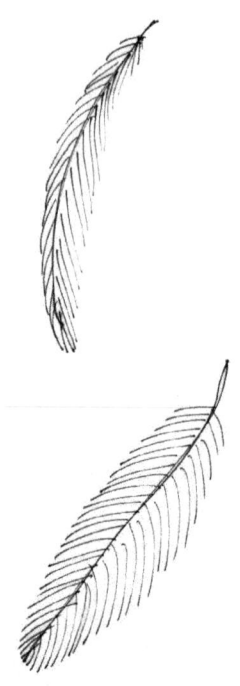

喜ビ苦シミ翻ル詩

日豪対訳アンソロジー

pleasant troubles

edited and translated by
Rina Kikuchi *with* Harumi Kawaguchi

菊地利奈編訳　　川口晴美監修

pleasant troubles
Recent Work Press
Canberra, Australia

Copyright © the authors and translators, 2018

ISBN: 9780648257974 (paperback)

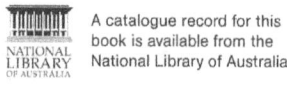
A catalogue record for this book is available from the National Library of Australia

All rights reserved. This book is copyright. Except for private study, research, criticism or reviews as permitted under the Copyright Act, no part of this book may be reproduced, stored in a retrieval system, or transmitted in any form by any means without prior written permission. Enquiries should be addressed to the publisher.

Cover illustration from *Cavorting with Time* © Jacqui Malins, 2018
Cover design: Recent Work Press
Set by Recent Work Press

recentworkpress.com

目次　Contents

序にかえて　Preface	1
三王発市街行　Three Kings to the City ジェン・クロフォード	4
風見鶏の家　The Weathercock ポール・マンデン	6
遁走曲〜アスペルガーと診断されて〜 Asperger's Diagnosis: A Fugue メリンダ・スミス	8
おやすみロジャーといっしょに旅していっしょに寝よう Join Roger on his Journey and Be Lulled to Sleep ジェン・クロフォード	12
雨のダンス I　Rain Dance—1 ニルーファー・ファナイヤン	16
愛と伝統　Love and Tradition エレン・ヴァン・ニーヴェン	20
崖っ縁に向きあって　Contemplating the Gap メリンダ・スミス	24
異世界で　In Other Universes シェーン・ストレンジ	28
ゴミ　Rubbish カッサンドラ・アサトン	30

スイカ　Watermelon カッサンドラ・アサトン	32
女たちの声はまだ届いていない Women Are Still Not Being Heard エレン・ヴァン・ニーヴェン	34
焔　Fire ニルーファー・ファナイヤン	36
ウィンチェスター大聖堂潜水員 The Winchester Diver ポール・マンデン	38
配管工　Plumber ポール・ヘザリントン	42
訳者注　Translator's Notes	44
詩人・訳者紹介　Biographies	48
初出一覧　Acknowledgements	56

序にかえて　Preface

　この小選集『喜ビ苦シミ翻ル詩〜日豪対訳詩集〜』には、オーストラリアゆかりの詩人の作品14篇を収めました。オーストラリアで生まれた方、育った方、教育を受けた方、就職された方、さまざまですが、みな、オーストラリアで詩作品が出版され、現在英語圏で活躍している詩人です。オーストラリアには詩の出版社が数多くあり、出版活動はもちろん、朗読会や詩祭等も活発におこなわれています。しかしながら、小さな出版社が多く、かれらの詩集や作品は、なかなか日本の市場にまで届いていません。オーストラリアで生まれ読まれている作品を、詩を愛する日本のみなさんにも届けたい、という想いから、本書は編まれました。

　ことのおこりは、2017年にキャンベラで開催された国際詩祭Poetry on the Moveでした。この詩祭に、新井高子、伊藤比呂美、川口晴美、山崎佳代子諸氏が出席、日英バイリンガル朗読会が開催されることになり、この朗読会にむけて『Poet to Poet: Contemporary Women Poets from Japan』(Recent Work Press, 2017)という現代日本女性詩人10名の作品を収録した対訳詩集が出版されました。その際私の共訳者となってくれたキャンベラ在住の詩人たちから、自分たちが現代日本語詩の世界にふれて詩的刺激を受けたように、今度は、自分たちの詩を日本へ届け、詩を媒体とした交流をさらに発展させたい、と相談を受けたのです。そういう意味では、英語から日本語に訳された『喜ビ苦シミ翻ル詩』は、日本語から英語に訳された『Poet to Poet』の返歌であるともいえます。

　ここに収められた詩人や詩は、「オーストラリア」を代表するものではなく、オーストラリアの多様性を伝える詩人・詩作品です。収録作品は、各詩人から「自分らしい」と思う作品を3篇選んでもらい、その中から、全体のバランスをみながら

1篇か2篇を私が選びました。オーストラリアの現代詩では、政治的な要素、あるいは自身の（政治的な、あるいは社会に向けての）主張がある詩が主流です。社会問題や環境問題はもちろん、女性、民族、社会的弱者への差別や蔑視などが、怒りや風刺、笑いとユーモアをもって表現tされることが多くあります。これらを明確なテーマとしてとりあげていない場合にも、これらが背景となった詩がほとんどです。その傾向を反映してか、各詩の「わたし」や「女」や「男」の声を通して、個人だけではなく、そのむこうに存在する社会を、世界を、感じていただけるような詩が、結果的には選ばれ収録されたように感じています。

　詩は訳せない、と言われることもありますが、訳せないことはありません。「詩は訳せない」と思われがちなのは、詩の訳である以上、訳されたものも「詩」であるべきだ、との考えがその根底にあるからではないか、と思います。つまりそれは、詩は訳せない、ということではなく、訳したものを日本語詩として完成させることが困難である、ということだと思うのです。英語詩を日本語に訳す（置き換える）ということであれば、詩を専門とする日本語話者の英文学者にも充分可能です。しかし、完成した「訳」が「和訳」としてだけではなく、「日本語詩」としても楽しみ読みうるものであるかは、また別の問題です。

　本書では、「英語詩の日本語訳」というだけでなく、原詩から離れすぎず、かつ、日本語詩としても楽しんでもらえる作品集にしたい、との想いから、『ことばを深呼吸』（東京書籍、2009年）の著者のおひとりである詩人の川口晴美さんに、監修作業をお願いしました。20年以上にわたって、詩の教室でたくさんの人の作品に寄り添い講師をつとめてきた川口さんに、言葉の選び方、句読点の打ち方、意味だけでなく音、ひとつの言葉から次の言葉への連想や飛躍、イメージを言語化することの重要性など、多くのことをご教授いただきました。私の訳と原詩を読み比べ、行間にあふれる言葉にならない想いを読み取ってくださり、ひとつの言葉を選ぶとき、ひとつの言葉を変更するとき、その理由や必要

性を、明確に明快に説明してくださった川口さんの真摯なご指導に、この場を借りて心から御礼申し上げます。

　また、川口さんと私の奮闘を応援し、自らの詩の背景を説明しながら、翻訳作業に協力してくれた、英語詩人のみなさん。なかでも、出版社Recent Work Press経営者であり、詩人のシェーン・ストレンジさんは、日本語が読めないにもかかわらず、対訳詩集という出版の在り方が詩の世界をこれからもっと広げていくことを信じて、本書を対訳詩集として出版してくださいました。本書の英語タイトル『pleasant troubles』は、喜び苦しむ翻訳作業にも通じると、シェーンさんが考えてくださったものです。その英語タイトルを『喜ビ苦シミ翻ル詩』と鮮やかに日本語に翻してくださったのは、川口さんです。本書が刊行できたのは、日英両言語の詩人のみなさんのおかげです。

　本書を通して、オーストラリア社会の多様性を反映する、多様な詩世界を、日本語訳詩を通して、あるいは、英語の原詩をちらちら見ながら、あるいは、読者のみなさんの自分なりの日本語訳詩を作ってみたりしながら、日本語で英語で、日英両言語で、それぞれに楽しんでいただければ幸いです。

　本書を手に取ってくださった読者のみなさんに、心からの感謝を込めて。

2018年6月　紅葉の美しいキャンベラにて

菊地利奈

Three Kings to the City

Jen Crawford

Why, when I catch the bus, do I share it with old women and not with old men? Are the old men still asleep or are they already at the shops? Did they walk? Did they drive? One of my grandfathers would only walk into town, walk from Balmoral to the city and back again in three hours. When he died of a heart attack fishing on the rocks, the doctor refused to go down to the beach, and the men who found him had to carry him up to the road. Once I dreamed I carried him on my back through a desert. Because he was dead he could no longer walk. I am not sure, in a heart attack, if the heart attacks or is attacked, is attack fishing now quietly with the tide, or perhaps the bus's old men are already dead. Perhaps they are driving regardless, like my other grandfather, who nearly died when, functionally blind with glaucoma, he drove into a sheep, and who nearly died when his ride-on mower rolled over on top of him at the bottom of a slope where the very long grass kept on growing.

三王発市街行

ジェン・クロフォード

バスに乗ったら、おじいさんはぜんぜん見当たらなくておばあさんばっかりなんだけど、どうしてだろう。おじいさんたちはみんなまだ寝ているのかな。それとも、もう街に着いちゃってる？　バスには乗らず歩いて行ったとか。そうじゃなきゃ車にしたのかもね。うちのおじいちゃんは、街へ行くときは必ず歩いていたなあ。バルモラルから街まで三時間、徒歩で往復してた。おじいちゃんは、岩場で釣りをしていたときに心臓発作で死んだんだった。医者にはそんなところまで降りて行けませんって断られたから、おじいちゃんを見つけた男のひとたちがおじいちゃんを道まで運び上げるしかなかったんだよね。一度、おじいちゃんをおぶって砂漠を歩く夢をみたことがあったっけ。おじいちゃんはもう死んじゃってるから、自力では歩けないもんね。心臓発作ってハート・アタックっていうけど、つまり心臓がアタックするの、アタックされるの、どっちなんだかよくわからない、フィッシィング・アタック、今は潮がひいて釣り場の波も静かになっているのかしら、もしかしてバスに乗るはずのおじいさんたちはみんな死んでしまったのかしら。いやいや、ちがうよね、おじいさんたちはみんな年のことなんか我関せず、自分で車を運転して行ったにきまってる、私のもうひとりのおじいちゃんみたいにね。こっちのおじいちゃんは緑内障でほとんど目が見えないのにトラクターを運転して、羊の群れにつっこんで、草の生い茂った坂の下に転げ落ちたあげく、さっきまで自分が運転してたトラクターにアタックされそうになったんだよ、おじいちゃんってば。

The Weathercock

Paul Munden

The iron weathervane needed new paint. Someone brought it down from the coach house roof—my father? braving that height, before he fell ill? (For me, the rooftop was the sky.) The cockerel perched on the lawn, and I scraped the flaking black from its north, south, east and west with a stiff wire brush, then daubed it with glistening enamel: scarlet beak and comb, gold feathers. I liked it there, left within reach, though it did no more than creak this way and that, bereft of the high winds that gave it true direction. Suddenly I see it's me, stuck there, gormless, aloof, waiting for my father to haul things back.

風見鶏の家

ポール・マンデン

鉄製の風見鶏は塗り直しが必要な頃だった。誰かが風見鶏を屋根から運び降ろした、たぶん父さんだったんじゃないかな、病気になる前はそのくらいの高さへっちゃらだったから(ぼくにとって、屋根は天空そのものだった)。雄鶏は芝生に休んで、北から南から東から西から剥がれていた黒片をぼくは固い金属ブラシで削り取り、輝くエナメルを塗り重ねた。深紅の嘴と鶏冠、金色の羽。真の方向を与えてくれる力強い風を奪われて、あっちこっちへきしむだけになっていたけれど、風見鶏がそこに、ぼくの手の届くところにある、それが嬉しかった。
不意に、気づく。これはぼく。こんなところで動けないまま、まぬけに、ぼんやりと、父さんがぜんぶ元通りにしてくれるのをただ待っている。

Asperger's Diagnosis: A Fugue

Melinda Smith

The cup finishes. I see. I look and look and hold on to it. It makes sense now. Cup. Hand. It *finishes*.

In *my* football draw there will be no elimination matches

I don't have Asperger's syndrome. I was terrified the horses and cows would fall off the hill

Here comes the Shoemaker-Levy 9! Here it comes!

We called for hours and hours, why didn't you answer?

I was being under a pyramid

The cup *finishes*. It makes sense now. I don't have Asperger's syndrome

David says I do but he's wrong. In *my* football draw the only elimination match will be the final

If there were no gravity we would all float up into the air and the oceans would leak away into space

We called for hours and hours, why didn't you answer?

I dreamed there was a big chicken in my room trying to eat my legs

遁走曲
～アスペルガーと診断されて～

メリンダ・スミス

カップの終わり。わかる。ぼくは見つめて、見つめて、手放さない。今、わかる。ここまでがカップ。ここからは手。終わり。

ぼくのフットボールマッチにはエリミネーション式トーナメントなんかない

ぼくはアスペルガーじゃない。丘から馬や牛が落っこちそうで怖かっただけ

シューメーカー・レヴィ第9彗星がぶつかる！　来るよ！

（ずっと何時間も呼んでたでしょ、なんで返事しなかったの？）

ぼくはね、ピラミッドにいたんだ

カップの終わり。今、わかる。僕はアスペルガーじゃない。

デビットは違うよって言うけど、間違っているのは彼のほうだよ。ぼくのフットボールマッチではね、エリミネーション式に排除されちゃうのは最終戦だけなんだから

もしも重力がなかったらぼくたちみんな空中に浮かんで、海の水はぜんぶ宇宙に流れ出ちゃうね

（ずっと何時間も呼んでたでしょ、なんで返事しなかったの？）

ぼくの脚を食べようとするおおきな鶏がぼくの部屋にいる夢をみたんだ

I don't have Asperger's syndrome. I look and look and hold onto it.

You say I do but you're wrong. In Me-land money, the notes start at seven cruzlaks

Elimination matches are REALLY unfair

Roman baths were a lot like our health clubs

We called for hours and hours, why didn't you answer?

I was terrified the horses and cows would fall

Cup. Hand. Cup. Hand. Asperger's syndrome is dumb.

I don't think there should be any more elimination matches, ever. I don't

The doctor says I do but he's a baddie!

The notes start at seven cruzlaks because there is a five cruzlak coin

We called for hours and hours, why didn't you answer?

The elephant bird was the biggest bird that ever lived

We called for hours and hours, why didn't you answer?

I knew where you were.

Parts of this poem ('the cup finishes' and 'I was terrified the horses and cows would fall off the hill') are from the book *Smiling at Shadows*, the story of autistic man Dane Waites and his family. (Junee Waites & Helen Swinbourne, HarperCollins 2001).

The cruzlak is a made-up currency invented by a young man I know who has Asperger's Syndrome.

ぼくはアスペルガーじゃない。ぼくは見つめて、見つめて、手放さない。
それは違うよっていうのが、間違いなんだよ。ぼくの国の貨幣は7クルツラック
　　からが紙幣なんだから
エリミネーション式トーナメントって、ほんっとにアンフェアだ
ローマ浴場って、健康ランドみたいなものだったんだよ
　（ずっと何時間も呼んでたでしょ、なんで返事しなかったの？）
丘から馬や牛が落っこちそうで怖かっただけ

カップ。手。カップ。手。アスペルガーなんかくそ食らえ。
もうこれ以上エリミネーション式トーナメントなんてやっちゃだめなんだ、絶対
　　に。やるもんか
ぼくが間違っているって医者は言うけど、あいつは悪いやつ！
紙幣は7クルツラックから始まるんだよ、だって5クルツラック硬貨があるんだもん
　（ずっと何時間も呼んでたでしょ、なんで返事しなかったの？）
エピオルニスは地上に存在したもっとも大きな鳥なんだ

　（ずっと何時間も呼んでたでしょ、なんで返事しなかったの？）
ぼくはみんながどこにいるか知っていたんだよ。

Join Roger on his Journey and Be Lulled to Sleep

Jen Crawford

My mum gave us this picture book by a Swedish behavioural scientist which is supposed to put the baby to sleep, and I gave it back. The rabbit is drawn in coloured pencil and he looks unwell, like someone who's been smoking a dozen cones a day since 2004 but hasn't slept since deciding to quit after breaking a rib coughing. The book warns you off reading the book to someone who's driving. Then the rabbit's mum takes him on a long journey to see Uncle Yawn. I do feel a bit sorry about uncles, but in the sense of general regret, not in the sense of personal responsibility. My memory of being hypnotised in 1988 by Bert Potter the communist free-love therapist who turned out to be a paedophile is surprisingly clear. There were a hundred people in the room, and nothing happened, except sun came in through the trees and the big bay windows onto the cushions and the groups of quiet, cuddled up people. My parents were taking the risk of love. Bert talked slowly about a beach, and the water line, and a stone, and a box. I breastfeed my son to sleep, which not everyone recommends. And sometimes

おやすみロジャーといっしょに旅して
いっしょに寝よう

ジェン・クロフォード

この絵本ならあなたの子もあっという間に寝かしつけられるわよと母親が差し出したのはスウェーデンの行動科学者が書いた絵本で魔法みたいだって評判らしいけどわたしはたたき返してやったわだってそこに描かれていた仔ウサギはどう見たってビョーキそれも毎日1ダースのマリファナきめて2004年からずっとそうしてたらついに咳き込んだ弾みに肋骨いっちゃってようやくクスリは止めることにしたもののそれ以来ぜんぜん眠れてないって顔なんだよしかも運転中の人には読み聞かせないでくださいって注意書きまである仔ウサギのロジャーは母ウサギに連れられてアクビオジサンって呼ばれてる親戚の男に会いに行く旅に出るんだけど「こどもと寝るオジサン」だよいいけどさペドかよペドなんじゃないのかよって思うのはぜったいわたしだけじゃないはず後になってペドフィリアだってばれたバート・ポターってやつは社会主義者で自由恋愛主義者でセラピストだった1988年にわたしはあいつに催眠術をかけられたんだってこともものすごく鮮やかに思い出してしまうあの部屋にいた100人もの人とか木漏れ日が差し込む大きな出窓に重なるクッションとか静かに抱きあっていた人々とかそれ以上のことは何もなかったけどあのときわたしをあそこに連れていった親たちはわたしという子どもの信頼を失うことになったかもしれなかったわたしの親はそういう賭けをしたんだあのときバートはただビーチについて波の描く線について小石について箱について話をしただけだったわたしは息子をおっぱいで寝かしつけるおっぱいで寝かしつけるというのはみんなに認めてもらえる方法じゃ

we go out into the backyard and talk to cockatoos or look for the moon instead, and everyone in the world is awake.

ないのはわかっているそれでいいのおっぱいをあげるかわりにたまに息子とふたりでいっしょに裏庭へ出て月を探したりまっしろなキバタンに話しかけたりするの世界中、すべての人、起きているよ。

Rain Dance—1

Niloofar Fanaiyan

The clinging filaments of her voice
permeate all things blue
as hearts fall and other shades are lost
before the horizon—

فرش آب در دامنهٔ آسمان انداختند،
تارهای آبی در ابریشم افق موج میزنند——

Farshe aab dar damaneye aseman andakhtan
tarhaye aaby dar abrishame ofogh m
meezanand—they have laid a carpet of wa
at the skirt of the mountain, webs of blue wa
within the silk of the horizon

silken threads rise
and rise again, the earth a loom with no back
and no front, an invisible frame.
A sprig of bluebells floats in her hair,

woven in the night
the weaving was accompanied by song
and dance—at one end of the bridge
یکی بود، یکی نبود
at the other end of the bridge
یکی بود، یکی نبود——

Yeky bood, yeky nabood—there was one,
and there was none (traditional Persian
introduction to oral fairy-tales)

雨のダンス I

　　　　　　　　　　　　　　　　ニルーファー・ファナイヤン

雫　寄りそって縒りあわさって地に結ばれて
たたんたたたん　静まりゆく心の　ひかりと影の
あわいは水平線に溶けて消え
水の歌声　すべてのものへと青く浸透する

فرش آب در دامنهٔ آسمان انداختند،　　　　　山裾に水の絨毯を敷く
تارهای آبی در ابریشم افق موج میزنند——　　青く波打つ蜘蛛の巣が絹糸の水平線におどる

絹の糸がのぼっていく
繰り返し　のぼるよ　地球という織り機には裏がなく
表もなく　透きとおって見えない枠
ブルーベルの青い花をアメノカミに飾って

夜のあいだに織られた
歌とダンスの織り込まれた布は
橋の片方のたもとに
یکی بود، یکی نبود　　　　　むかしむかし　片方にはあり　他方にはない
橋のもう片方のたもとにも
دوبن یکی, دوب یکی　　　　　むかしむかし　片方にはあり　他方にはない

چشمهای دیروز در آبی دریا،
باران فردا در آبی هوا –

Chashmhaye deerooz dar aabiye darya, barane farda dar aabiye havaa—the eyes of yesterday are in the blue of the sea, the rain of tomorrow is in the blue of the sky

and today is lost in the air between.

The moon flutes a winding breeze,

disrupts the many shades of blue,

and the rain swings around the loom—

باران میرقصد و میپرسد:
کدام آب است و کدام هوا،
کدام زمین است و کدام فضا؟

Baran meeraghsad va meeporsad: kodam aab ast va kodam havaa, kodam zameen ast va kodam fazaa—the rain dances and asks: which is water and which is air, which is earth and which is space?

Water and air whisper against the skin

of her hand, her feet, her face.

She hums and whirls,

sky and sea,

she is blue.

چشمهای دیروز در آبی دریا،
باران فردا در آبی هوا –

昨日の目には海の青
明日の雨には空の青

そうしてふたつの青のあわいへと今日は消えゆく
月は渦巻くそよ風を吹いて奏でながら
幾層もの青の影を攪拌する
雨は織り機のまわりをスイングして踊っている

باران میرقصد و میپرسد:
کدام آب است و کدام هوا،
کدام زمین است و کدام فضا؟

雨は踊り雨は聞く
どっちが水でどっちが空気
どっちが地上でどっちが天

水と空気が　雨の肌に　囁く

雨の　手に　足に　顔に　触れて　囁く

雨はハミングしてくるくるくるりまわり続ける

空よ　海よ

雨　そなたは青い

Love and Tradition

Ellen van Neerven

rising sea
takes and
breaks into backyards
to trouble families

we cannot live
with the seas in our bellies
we cannot rest
with the sea at our legs

the tide
is coming
to stroke
our dead

we want to know
who unplugged
our island
of childhood

愛と伝統

エレン・ヴァン・ニーヴェン

海がせりあがる

裏庭にまで及び

波くだけて

家人たちに困難をもたらす

わたしたち　お腹に海を抱え

生きていくことができない

わたしたち　足を海に浸され

休息することができない

潮が

満ちる

亡き者たちに

触れて波打つ

わたしたちは知りたい

誰がわたしたちの

あの子ども時代の島の

栓を抜いたのか

island

of love and tradition

let them see

what has gone under

島

愛と伝統の島

見るがいい

流れ過ぎ去ったすべてを

Contemplating the Gap

i.m. Don Ritchie

Melinda Smith

Every story stumbles
in its own way. All so far
from here and from each other.
The funnel has a wide mouth.
But one by one they slide down it to teeter
on the lip of this one exit,
staring at the heave of the sea, breath
beaten from them by the cliff wind.
You can't just sit there and watch
through your window. Can I
help you in some way?
A hundred and sixty times and I've never
lost one. Sometimes they come
for a cuppa afterwards. They
tell me things. They tell me
you feel the pull in your guts
and your giddy head, there is an urge

崖っ縁に向きあって
～ドン・リッチーの思い出に～

メリンダ・スミス

どんな物語も躓くときがある
すべては遠く
ここから遠く、互いに遠く
だけど漏斗の口は広くあいていて
ひとり、またひとり、その縁へふらふら来てそれぞれの物語を
滑り落としてしまう、たったひとつの出口へ向かって
ふるえ波打つ海を見つめながら
息は崖の風に打ち砕かれてしまう
ここにただ座って窓から眺めているだけ、なんて
無理だ。「なにか僕に
できることはないかい？」
160回そう言って一度も
ひとりも、失わなかった。そうするとたまに
うちにお茶を飲みにくる人もいる、彼らは
語るんだ、頭がぐらぐらして
はらわたが引っ張られるような感じがして

to laugh and an urge

to launch into the maw,

to make gravity finish all at once

the dirty dragging work it started the day

you were born. They tell me

you only feel vertigo

when you don't want to fall.

Can I help you in some way?

Most of them come back with No.

I'm a salesman though. No

is a beginning.

This poem is in memory of Don Ritchie, an ordinary man with a job in sales who lived for many years near 'The Gap' at Sydney's South Head, a popular suicide spot due to the high cliffs overlooking the ocean. Mr Ritchie took it upon himself to start a conversation with anyone he happened to see who looked like they might be thinking about jumping.

大笑いしたい衝動にかられるって
体の底に着地しなきゃならない気分になるって
重力をいますぐ一気に終わらせてしまいたいんだ、
生まれた瞬間から始まる重力に汚れた生を終わらせたいんだ、って
彼らは語る
目眩を感じるのは
ほんとうは落ちたくないときだけ
「なにか僕にできることはないかい？」
返事はたいてい「ない」
だけど僕はセールスマンだからね、「ない」
それはすべての始まりなんだ

In Other Universes

Shane Strange

the parts actors play are their real lives. They do not know why they speak to themselves in dramatic monologue. The people you slept with have traded places with the people you wished you'd slept with. The dog you owned as a child appears on TV as a Sunday morning cartoon, beloved by children everywhere, and lives in the memory of adults as nostalgia warm and pure. Narrative time gawps at an empty plain and waits for movements of the sun. Unbroken attention spans hold on and hold on and hold on... In other universes, each conclusion is the right one. All suspicions have been confirmed. Each decision has been made, each chance taken. Each possibility, no matter how outlandish, is achieved. Each sperm and egg are children. Each bomb dropped does not explode. Every indiscretion has been discovered. Every daydream lives and aches and draws pay. In other universes the molecules comprising the body differ by one. Cancer can be a good thing. Gods pray to humans, and humans pray to dust. In other universes, the fears you wake to have manifested, or remain ideal. However, their sum never diminishes or expands. In all universes, this is a constant.

異世界で

シェーン・ストレンジ

キャストたちが演じているのは彼らの現実の人生だ。彼らはわけもわからず自分自身についてドラマティックなモノローグで語る。ねちゃった相手はみんな、ねたいなって夢見ていた人にすり替わっている。こどもの頃に飼っていた犬は、日曜の朝のテレビアニメに登場してすべてのこどもたちに愛され、大人たちのハートウォーミングでピュアでノスタルジックな思い出の中、生きている。物語の時間はからっぽの草原でとまっていて、太陽が動くのを待ってる。集中力はとぎれることがない、ずっとずっとずーっと……続く。異世界では、すべての結論が正しい結論。すべての疑念は晴れる。決定はすべてきちんと下されて、どんなチャンスだってつかめる。どの可能性も、それがどれほど途方もないことだったとしても関係ない、達成される。すべての精子と卵子がこどもになる。投下された爆弾はひとつとして爆発しない。隠されたすべてのことが明らかになる。夢見たすべてを本当に生きて、痛みもあるし、仕事の対価は払われる。異世界の体を構成する分子は、ひとつずつ違っているだけ。癌はいいものになれる。神々は人間に祈り、人間は塵に祈る。異世界では、きみを眠りから目覚めさせてしまう恐怖は、現実化するか、空想の中にとどまるか、どちらか。だけど、恐怖の総量は、減りも増えもしないんだ。どんな異世界でも恐怖の総量は、一定で変わらない。

Rubbish

Cassandra Atherton

It is Tuesday and I am dreaming that I live inside the trashcan on your Apple MacBook screen. Bottom right. Lid slightly ajar. My head popping up at intervals, not to offer you advice, but to ask you why you left me. You have three reasons but I can't hear what they are. The trashcan graphic is too solid and the sound waves ricochet off the crenellations. Facets. Indentations. You have to type your responses and drag them to me so I can read them. I wait for you in the trashcan. I wait for your mouse to lift me up and make me an icon. I want to be a square pink button with a harp sound when you click on me. I want to shimmer and pulse so you recognise me. I want you to constantly press on me. Double click. (Is there are triple or quadruple click?) I want your mouse to slide over me as I sit. Patiently. Singing Kumbayah and toasting pink marshmallows. Listening for you. You never let anyone else use your computer. No foreign fingers have ever touched the keys so I feel safe. I am only yours. I am the only trashcan you have ever used. I wonder if you have ever been unfaithful. If you have used other computers when I am sleeping. If you prefer other trashcans to mine. I worry every day that you will go to 'Empty Trash' and I will disappear.

ゴミ

カッサンドラ・アサトン

今日は火曜日。俺はあんたのゴミ箱の中で暮らす夢をみている。あんたのマックブックの画面右下にあるゴミ箱の中。蓋は少しだけ開いている。ときどきちょろっと顔を出すけど、別に何か役に立つようなことを言おうとしているわけじゃない、俺はただ、なんで俺を捨てたんだってあんたに聞きたいのさ。理由は3つあるってあんたは言うけど、ゴミ箱の中の俺には聞こえない。ゴミ箱の表面は固くてデコボコで、どんな音波も跳ね返しちまうからな。凸凹。凹凸なんだ。だから返事をタイプして、このゴミ箱にドラッグしてくれよ、俺、読むからさ。ずっとゴミ箱の中で俺は待っている。あんたがそのマウスで俺を持ちあげてホーム画面に戻してくれるのを、待っているんだ。俺の四角いアイコンがあんたの好きなピンク色になって、あんたにクリックされるとあんたの好きなハープの音が鳴るってふうになればいいんだけどなあ。ぶるぶると脈打つようにアイコンが揺れていたら、あんたも俺に気づくだろう？ずっとあんたに触っていてほしいんだ。ダブルクリックされたい（トリプルクリック、クアトロクリックだって大歓迎）。あんたのマウスに触ってもらえることを念じながら、俺はここに座っている。忍耐強く、待っている。ゴスペルのクンバヤを歌い、ピンクのマシュマロをトーストして、あんたの声が聞こえてくるんじゃないかっていつも耳を澄ませている。あんたは自分のマックを他人には使わせたりしない、このキーボードに触るのはあんただけだから、俺は安心している。俺はあんただけのものだ。あんただけが使うこのゴミ箱、ここに俺はいる。もしかして、あんたは俺を裏切ったのか？俺が寝ている隙に他のパソコンを使ったりしたか？俺というゴミ箱じゃない、よそのゴミ箱に、ドラッグしてみようなんて思ったりしていたら、俺はどうすりゃいいんだよ。あんたがそのうち「ゴミ箱を空にする」をクリックして、俺が消えちまったら、どうすればいい？毎日そんなことばっかり気に病んでいる。

Watermelon

Cassandra Atherton

After 85 days, I gave birth to a watermelon. It wasn't easy, a full-term jubilee watermelon is forty pounds and this one was delivered breech. When my water broke, it pooled on the floorboards beneath my bare feet. You didn't realise it would travel under the wood and warp the grain. You'd only find that out the following day when you brought the watermelon home; you could feel the edges of the board curving under your toes. By the time you got me to the hospital, I was dilated ten centimetres and the nurse said it was too late for an epidural. But the melon's rind was slick and helped me squeeze it down the birth canal. When I finally pushed it out, I held it in my arms, stroking the skin. 'It's perfect,' you said sniffing its head, 'smells so sweet'. It takes a while to stitch me up, so I stay in the hospital while you take the watermelon home. You ring me from the kitchen, swollen boards under your feet, the long-bladed knife in your hand. 'Next time, let's try for a cantaloupe', you say.

スイカ

カッサンドラ・アサトン

スイカを産んだのは85日後。楽じゃなかったよ。完熟したスイカは大玉で20キロもあって、おまけに逆子だったんだ。破水して、キッチンに立っていた私の足元には水がたまっていった。たまった水は床下まで染みて、床板を反らすだろうって、あなた、思いもしなかったんだね。翌日になってスイカを家に連れ帰ったあなたの足裏が、反り返ってしまった床板に触れてやっと気づいたんだよね。病院に到着したとき、あなたに運び込まれた私の開口部はもう10センチも開いちゃってて無痛分娩の麻酔は間に合いませんって。それでもスイカの表皮はつるんと滑らかで、産道から押し出しやすかった。ついに産み終えた私は、両腕に抱いてやさしく皮をなでてあげたんだ。あなたは、「五体満足、完璧！」だなんて言いながらつむじに鼻を近づけ「甘い匂いがする」って。そのあと会陰縫合をしなくちゃならない私は病院に残り、あなたはスイカと家に帰った。それでキッチンで、水浸しになって反り返った床板を踏んで、出刃包丁を持ったまま、あなたは私に電話してきたんだよ、「次はさ、メロンにしよう」って。

Women Are Still Not Being Heard

For Ms Dhu

Ellen van Neerven

women are still not being heard
our bodies ignored
crimes against us approved
sister spoke up
it collapsed her kidney
custody, over custodianship
children taken, and land
weeping and lonely
no more women unheard behind the wall
no more women dead over unpaid fines
no more women dead by men
we are shaving and craving the world

女たちの声はまだ届いていない
～ミズ・ドゥーの死に寄せて～

エレン・ヴァン・ニーヴェン

女のことばはまだ聞き届けられていない

わたしたちの体は無価値に扱われ

わたしたちへの犯罪は許容される

語ろうと立ち上がる女は

内臓ごと潰され

拘束され監視される

こどもたちを奪われ土地を奪われ

泣いてひとりきり

女が壁の向こうに押しやられ声を聞き届けられないなんてもうたくさん

女が罰金を払えないだけで死ぬはめになるなんてもうたくさん

女たちが男たちに殺されるのはもうたくさん

わたしたちが刈り整える世界を渇望する

Fire

Niloofar Fanaiyan

the sequined edge of her gypsy skirt,
early morning rays,
brushes the hammered sides of a copper pot—
she lights the stack of wood beneath and casts the spices into
   its depths,
growing flames caress a rounded belly
reflecting their dance, a musical shushing
mingling with the louder light—
she reaches for a wooden spoon and stirs
the spices slowly cracking in the heat,
each one is a shade of fire,
a web of warmth of far-reaching strands—
from the first taste the end is clear,
every atom is touched
and cast into the sun

焔

　　　　　　　　　　　　ニルーファー・ファナイヤン

スパンコールに縁取られて閃くジプシースカート

早朝の太陽光線

軽やかに触れられて赤銅色の鍋の打刻された模様が燦めき

下に積み重ねた薪に火をつけて女は鍋の深くへとスパイスを振り入れる

おおきく育ちゆく炎が赤銅のまるいおなかをやさしく撫で

炎のダンスを反射させて、シュッシューッと奏でる音は

さらにおおきな輝きと混じりあう

女はおもむろに差し伸ばした手に木べらを取り　ゆっくりと

熱くはねるスパイスの粒をかきまわす

ひとつひとつが異なる炎の影を生み出してゆく

遠い向こう岸のあたたかな熱はレース状につながりひろがって

最初のひとくちでどうなるかは明らか

ひとつひとつの原子は触れあい

太陽のただなかに振り入れられる

The Winchester Diver

i.m. William Walker (1869–1918), who saved the cathedral with his own two hands

Paul Munden

For five years, daily, he seals himself
into a monastic, rubberized suit
with only his two pink frond-like hands
protruding. His feet are lead weights.
His bulbous, brass-cased head
is pure Science Fiction. The Lagoon Man.
He spits on the eye-piece to prevent it misting,
more out of habit than to any effect.
Within a minute he's working blind,
his own slow progress stirring
further sediment in the lugubrious drift
right under the foundations. The sound
of the cathedral choir wafts down
but there's no hint of what permeates
his brain throughout the numbing routine.
His sledgehammer sledgehammers on. Blocks

ウィンチェスター大聖堂潜水員
〜自らの両腕で大聖堂を救ったウィリアム・ウォーカー(1869-1918)に捧げる〜

ポール・マンデン

五年の間、来る日も来る日も、男は
ゴム製の修道服に身を包んだ
薄桃色の両手のひらだけそこから突き出させて。
鉛の重りをつけた足で。
まんまるい真鍮ヘルメットを被ると
もうまったくSF。〈半魚人〉でしかない。
ゴーグル部分に男がつばをつけるのは曇らないようにするため、
とはいえ単なる習慣だから効果のほどは不明。
一分もしないうちに闇の中での作業になってしまう、
ゆっくりゆっくりやっていくしかない
悲惨な泥濘と化した場所に埋もれながら堆積物を掻き出す、
大聖堂の土台の下。聖歌隊の
音楽が流れ着く
けれど果てしない作業に麻痺した男の耳には
届かない
ハンマーを打ち続ける。水浸しの

of water-logged peat are packed into bucket
after bucket until at last his fingers rasp
against shingle, a good moment to surface
for a smoke—nicotine to protect him
from the diseased, graveyard swamp
in which he works.

Is that a tease, like the walrus moustache?
Looking at the photographs is going
back with him, shoring up each trench
with a similar commitment.
Down come sacks of cement to lug
into place. Calmly, he slits every throat
and pumps pressurized grout into the cracks
between each slumped and saturating corpse.
The shifting ground becomes a monolith
fit to take the strain of a millennium.
As he starts to tire, he jerks the lifeline
and lets a shot of air billow
around his midriff, forcing him up again
into a world almost as dim.

泥炭は次から次へバケツいっぱいになって
指がこけら板に到達すれば、ようやく休憩のタイミング、
一服だ、ニコチンは
潜るしかないこの病んだ墓地の汚泥から
男を守ってくれるという。

あれは冗談だったのか？ ちょび髭の冗談みたいな彼のセイウチづらとおんなじで？
写真を見つめながら、汚泥の中へと潜って行く
彼とともに、危険な壕のひとつひとつを
同じ命がけの献身で支えるんだ。
降りてくるセメント袋を
力を尽くして正しい位置に据える。
静かに、すべての袋の喉を切り裂いて
加圧した空隙補充材を流し込む、ぐったりして
水に膨張したぬけがら、なきがらの隙間に詰め込んでいく。
揺らいだ大聖堂の地は一枚岩になり
千年は大丈夫。
疲れ果て、命綱をぐいっと引けば
地上の空気に射ぬかれる上半身は膨らんで波打って
また地下と同じ
ほのぐらい世界に投げ捨てられている。

Plumber

for PM

Paul Hetherington

After his poetry reading—passionate, exhausting, with students standing to applaud—he overheard the deputy principal saying "why do we pay them when they do it for love? Our toilet still isn't fixed." He retrained at the local technical college, mounting his plumber's certificate next to a Book of the Year award. He offered a combined service to schools in his district: "Plumbing attended to; reading or talk thrown in", charging for the first and offering the second at a reduced fee. Principals and English teachers were keen—all enjoyed poetry with the heating at full bore, knowing their cisterns didn't leak. In a few years he became a national figure: his poems were on the curriculum, his work was praised as fluid and well controlled. When he died unexpectedly on a school tour there was a spanner on top of a manuscript in his room, and in his pocket a manual on guttering.

配管工
～ＰＭに捧ぐ～

ポール・ヘザリントン

朗読会の終わり——情熱をもって魂を燃やし尽くし、学生たちが立ち上がって大喝采の拍手をしながら取り囲んでくれた、まさにその瞬間——「なんで詩人なんかに金を払うんだ、好きで朗読してるんだろ？　我々の学校のトイレはまだ直っていないのに」と言い放った副校長の声が、彼の耳に入ったのだ。彼は地元の技術学校に入学し直し、配管工としての資格証明書をブック・オブ・ザ・イヤーの賞状と並べて掲げることにした。で、そのふたつのセットサービスを地区の学校に提供。「配管修理承ります、朗読や講義も」。ひとつめの仕事に代金を払えば、ふたつめの仕事は割引料金にする。校長も文学教師も大歓迎——自分たちのタンクが水漏れする心配はないのだから、タンク熱を利用したセントラルヒーティングをガンガンにきかせて、詩を心ゆくまで味わえた。数年後、彼は国民的存在となり、詩は教科書に載った。彼の詩の言葉は滞ることなく流れ、見事にコントロールされている。学校訪問中に彼が急逝したとき、残されたのは、彼の部屋の原稿の上に置かれたスパナと、ポケットの中の排水溝洗浄マニュアルだった。

訳者注　Translator's Notes

「三王発市街行」
――三王 (Three Kings) は、オークランド (ニュージーランド) 郊外の町の名前。タイトルは、三王からオークランドへ行くバスの表示。

「遁走曲～アスペルガーと診断されて～」
――「カップの終わり (the cup finishes)」と「丘から馬や牛が落っこちそうで怖かっただけ (I was terrified the horses and cows would fall off the hill)」は、『影に微笑んで――ある母の苦しみと喜びに満ちた旅 (Smiling at Shadows : a Mother's Journey through Heartache and Joy)』(Junee and Dane Waites, with Helen Swinburne, HarperCollins, 2001) からの引用。この本は、自閉症の息子を持った母ジュニー・ウェイツと息子のディンのふたりが、ヘレン・スウィンバーンの監修のもとに書いた、ディンの成長物語。
――クルツラック (Cruzlak) は、詩人の知るアスペルガー症候群の男の子がつくった貨幣単位。

「おやすみロジャーといっしょに旅していっしょに寝よう」
――ロジャーとは、世界的ベストセラーとなったカール＝ヨハン・エリーン著の絵本『おやすみ、ロジャー　魔法のぐっすり絵本』(2015) の主人公のウサギの男の子の名前。
――バート・ポター (Bert Potter, 1925–2012) は、ニュージーランドのオークランドでセンターポイントという新興宗教コミュニティーを創設した人。1991

年、未成年者への性的暴行の疑いで逮捕され、1992年に3歳半の女の子を
ふくむ、5人の未成年少女への強制わいせつ行為で懲役7年の刑を受けた。
── キバタン（cockatoo）は、オーストラリアに広く分布する50センチほどの大型オウ
ウム。王冠のようにひろがる、鮮やかな黄色の冠羽と真っ白なボディが特徴。

「雨のダンスⅠ」
── 挿入されている外国語の詩行は、ペルシア語。
──「むかしむかし　片方にはあり　他方にはない」は、日本語の「むかしむかし
　　あるところに」にあたる、ペルシア語のおとぎ話のはじまりの定型。

「崖っ縁に向きあって」
── 長年生命保険会社のセールスマンとして勤務したドン・リッチー氏（1925-
　　2012）に捧げられた詩。リッチー氏は、シドニーの「ギャップ」と呼ばれる絶
　　壁から、50メートルしか離れていない、ワトソン湾に面した家で半世紀近く
　　暮らした。「ギャップ」は自殺の名所でもあり、リッチー氏は自宅のリビングの
　　窓から崖っぷちに歩いていく人を見ると、声をかけるようになったという。
　　リッチー氏は、自殺しようとしていた160名もの人を引きとめ命を救ったと
　　して表彰された。

「ゴミ」
── 原詩では、この詩の語り手「I」と「you」の性別は限定されない。しかし日本語
　　では、性別を限定しない訳は困難であることから、ふたりの男女（あるいは男

男・女女）関係を想定したうえで訳すことにした。ピンクのアイコンになってハープを奏でたい、と希望する「I」を女性だと仮定することは容易であるが、川口氏の提案により、「I」を女性としたバージョンと、「I」を男性としたバージョンの両方をつくったうえで、ここでは男性案を採択することとした。

「女たちの声はまだ届いていない」

— ミズ・ドゥー（Ms Dhu）は、オーストラリア先住民の女性で、2014年、罰金が払えずにいたため、警察に拘留され、拘置所で体調不良を訴えたが認められず不当な死を遂げた。オーストラリア先住民（主に男性）に対してこのようなことが頻繁に起きていること、ミズ・ドゥーが22歳の若い女性だったこと、死に至るほどの体調不良と苦痛を申し出たにもかかわらず適切な対応がなされなかったこと、たった3日間の拘留のうちに亡くなったことなどから、警察の不適切な処置と先住民に対する差別とが指摘され、先住民をはじめとする多くの人々の反響を呼んだ。

「ウィンチェスター大聖堂潜水員」

— イギリス南部のハンプシャー州にあるウィンチェスター大聖堂は、11世紀に創建された。14世紀末から16世紀にかけて建設された奥行き170メートルもの身廊は、イギリス国内最長のものとして有名。

— 1900年代に入り、ウィンチェスター大聖堂の土台に亀裂が発生し、大聖堂全体が沈下する恐れが生じた。川辺の泥炭地帯に建てられていたため、土地が浸水し、大聖堂の沈下が危ぶまれた。建築技師の指導により、建物の土台の4メートル下にコンクリートを流し込み安定させることになった。その作業に、軍隊で潜水員として活躍した、ウィリアム・ウォーカー（William Walker,

1869–1918）が選ばれた。ウォーカー氏は大聖堂の基礎の下、真っ暗闇の泥水に、5年間にわたり毎日6時間ひとりで潜り、手探りで大聖堂修復作業をおこなった。ウィンチェスター大聖堂の救世主として、イギリス王室ビクトリア勲章が授与された。大聖堂敷地内に彼の銅像がある。
— 詩の歴史的背景には、大聖堂の修復作業に加え第一次世界大戦中のイギリスがある。

「配管工」
— この詩が捧げられているPMとは、本書に詩が収録されている、詩人のポール・マンデン（Paul Munden）をさす。

詩人・訳者紹介 Biographies

カッサンドラ・アサトン（Cassandra Atherton）

アデレード生まれ、メルボルン育ちの散文詩人・研究者。2014年上智大学客員研究員。2016年ハーバード大学客員研究員。現在、ディーキン大学准教授としてクリエィティブ・ライティングを教える。モナッシュ大学日本研究センター客員教員。オーストラリアの文学誌『Westerly』の詩部門の編集者でもある。最近の散文詩集に『ピカドン』(*Pika-don*, Mountains Brown Press, 2018)、『発掘』(*Exhumed*, Grand Parade Poets, 2015)、『トレース』(*Trace*, Finlay Lloyd, 2015)がある。

ジェン・クロフォード（Jen Crawford）

アオテアロア（ニュージーランドのマオリ語名）に生まれ、フィリピン、オーストラリア、シンガポールで暮らし、現在キャンベラ大学国際詩学研究所(International Poetry Studies Institute)准教授。文学作品における異文化表現・表象、「詩」と「土地」のつながりに着目して文学研究をおこなっている。『オニカッコウ』(*Koel*, Cordite Books, 2016)、『地衣は石を愛す』(*Lichen Loves Stone*, Tinfish Press, 2016)など、8冊の詩集・チャップブック（小冊子）がある。

ニルーファー・ファナイヤン（Niloofar Fanaiyan）

ペルシア系オーストラリア作家・詩人。これまでアメリカ、オーストラリア、オランダ、タンザニアで暮らし、現在イスラエル在住。2016年、キャンベラ大学の研究員となり、博士号を取得。第一詩集『トランジット』(*Transit*, Recent Work Press, 2016)にて、キャンベラクリティックサークル文学賞詩部門(Canberra Critics Circle Literary Award)を受賞。

ポール・ヘザリントン（Paul Hetherington）

アデレード生まれ。現在、キャンベラ大学国際詩学研究所（International Poetry Studies Institute）の教授としてクリエイティブライティングを教えている。『イカロス』（*Íkaros*, Recent Work Press, 2017)、散文詩集『夾竹桃にさす月明かり』（*Moonlight on Oleander: Prose poems*, UWA Publishing, 2018）など、13冊の詩集・散文詩集、及び6冊のチャップブック（小冊子）がある。2014年、西オーストラリアプレミアブック賞詩部門（Western Australian Premier's Book Award）を受賞。

川口晴美（Harumi Kawaguchi）

福井県小浜市生まれ。東京在住。1985年に第一詩集『水姫』を出版。いくつかの大学で創作の授業を担当し、社会人向けの詩の講座では講師を務めている。詩集『半島の地図』（2009）で第10回山本健吉文学賞受賞。詩集『*Tiger is here.*』（2015）で第46回高見順賞受賞。アンソロジーの企画・編集なども手がける。

菊地利奈（Rina Kikuchi）

滋賀大学准教授、オーストラリア国立大学客員研究員、キャンベラ大学客員研究員。1920年〜40年代の日本語女性詩を研究。日英バイリンガルアンソロジー『*Poet to Poet: Contemporary Women Poets from Japan*』（Recent Work Press, 2017）の編訳者をジェン・クロフォードと共に務めた。

ポール・マンデン（Paul Munden）

イギリス南部に生まれ、北部のヨークシャーにて、長年、クリエイティブライティングの指導をする国立機関（National Association of Writers in Education）のディレ

クターを務めた。その後、映画監督スタンリー・キューブリック(Stanley Kubrick, 1928-99)のリサーチャーとして文学作品教授係を担当したり、スイスのブリティッシュ・カウンシルにてカンファレンス・ポエトを務めたりした後、2015年から3年間、キャンベラ大学にて、国際詩祭Poetry on the Moveのディレクターを務めた。ローレンス・スターンの長編『トラストラム・シャンディ』をベースとした『星標』(*Asterisk*, Smith|Doorstop, 2011)、『半音色』(*Chromatic*, UWA Publishing, 2017)など、5冊の詩集がある。オウィディウスの生誕2000年を祝うアンソロジー『変身物語―21世紀の詩人からオウィディウスへの返歌』(*Metamorphic: 21st century poets respond to Ovid*, Recent Work Press, 2017)では、ネッサ・オマホニー(Nessa O'Mahony)と共に編者を務めた。

メリンダ・スミス(Melinda Smith)
オーストラリア・ニューサウスウェールズ州のウェリントンで生まれ、同州のオレンジで育つ。オーストラリア国立大学の法学部及び日本研究科卒。在学中の1992年、交換留学生として関西大学で学ぶ。法律家、公務員、ITコンサルタント、大学教員などをしながら、イギリス・ケンブリッジ、アメリカ・ワシントンDCで暮らした。6冊の詩集のうち、『ドラッグしてロック解除／緊急電話』(*Drag down to unlock or place an emergency call*, Pitt Street Poetry, 2013)は2014年オーストラリア総理大臣文学賞(Australian Prime Minister's Literary Award)を受賞した。作品はイタリア語やインドネシア語など複数の言語に翻訳されている。現在キャンベラ在住。キャンベラタイムズの詩の元選者。

シェーン・ストレンジ（Shane Strange）
オーストラリアのメルボルン生まれ、クイーンズランド州育ち。出版社や銀行勤めを経て、現在キャンベラ大学教員。過去に日系の銀行に勤めたこともある。詩と散文を書き、出版社Recent Work Pressを経営。

エレン・ヴァン・ニーヴァン（Ellen van Neerven）
クイーンズランド州南東部のオーストラリア先住民族ユガンバ族の詩人・作家。詩集に『コンフォートフード』（*Comfort Food*, University of Queensland Press, 2016）。短編集『熱と光』（*Heat and Light*, University of Queensland Press, 2014）にて、2015年ドビー文学賞（Dobbie Literary Award）をはじめとする複数の文学賞を受賞。

Cassandra Atherton was born in Adelaide and grew up in Melbourne. She was a Harvard Visiting Scholar in English in 2016, a Visiting Scholar at Sophia University in 2014 and is an affiliate of the Monash Japanese Studies Centre. She is a prose poet, poetry editor of Westerly magazine and Associate Professor of Writing and Literature at Deakin University. Her most recent books of prose poetry are *Exhumed*, *Trace* and *Pika-don*.

Jen Crawford is an Assistant Professor of Writing within the Centre for Creative and Cultural Research at the University of Canberra. She was born in Aotearoa/New Zealand, and has also lived in the Philippines, Australia, and Singapore. Her critical writing focuses on the poetics of place and on cross-cultural engagements in various literary contexts. She is the author of eight poetry books and chapbooks, including *Koel* (Cordite Books, 2016) and *Lichen Loves Stone* (Tinfish Press, 2016).

Niloofar Fanaiyan is a Persian-Australian writer and poet who has lived in the U.S., Australia, the Netherlands, Tanzania and Israel. She was the 2016 Donald Horne Research Fellow at the Centre for Creative and Cultural Research, University of Canberra, where she obtained her PhD. She received the Canberra Critics Circle Literary Award for Poetry for her first book of poems titled *Transit* (RWP, 2016).

Paul Hetherington was born in Adelaide, and has since lived in Perth and Canberra. He has published 13 collections of poetry and prose poetry – including, most recently *Íkaros* (RWP, 2017) and *Moonlight on Oleander: Prose poems* (UWAP, 2018)—along with six poetry chapbooks. He won the 2014 Western Australian Premier's Book Award (poetry) and was shortlisted for the 2018 international *Aesthetica* Creative Writing Competition (poetry), the 2017 Kenneth Slessor Prize for Poetry and the 2017 International Bridport Prize (Flash Fiction). He leads the International Poetry Studies Institute (IPSI) in the Faculty of Arts and Design at the University of Canberra and is Professor of Writing there.

Harumi Kawaguchi was born in Obama, Fukui Prefecture, Japan. Her first poetry book, *Water Princess* (水姫) was published in 1985. She has been teaching creative writing at multiple universities and has been lecturing in poetry writing for more than two decades. Her tenth poetry collection, *Map of the Peninsula* (半島の地図, 2009) won the 10th Yamamoto Kenkichi Literary Prize and *Tiger is Here* (*Tiger is here*, 2015) won the 46th Takami Jun Poetry Prize. Apart from her own poetry books, she is an author of a poetry writing book and an editor of various poetry anthologies.

Rina Kikuchi is an associate professor at Shiga University, Japan. She has been a visiting fellow at the Australian National University since 2016 and at the University of Canberra since 2017, conducting her research on modern and contemporary Japanese women's poetry, which includes poetry translation. She has co-translated Japanese poetry with various Australian poets, which were published in *Poet to Poet: Contemporary Women Poets from Japan* (eds.by Rina Kikuchi & Jen Crawford, Recent Work Press, 2017).

Paul Munden was born on the south coast of England, and has spent much of his life in North Yorkshire, as Director of the UK's National Association of Writers in Education. He was reader for Stanley Kubrick from 1988–98, and worked as conference poet for the British Council in Switzerland. In 2015 he took up a position as Postdoctoral Research Fellow at the University of Canberra, where he is also Program Manager for the International Poetry Studies Institute (IPSI), running the annual Poetry on the Move festival. He has published five collections including *Asterisk* (Smith | Doorstop, 2011), based on Shandy Hall, former home of Laurence Sterne, and *Chromatic* (UWA Publishing, 2017). He is co-editor with Nessa O'Mahony of *Metamorphic: 21st century poets respond to Ovid* (Recent Work Press, 2017).

Melinda Smith was born in Wellington and grew up in Orange, both country towns in New South Wales, Australia. She has degrees in Japanese Studies and Law from the Australian National University in Canberra, and spent 1992 on exchange at Kansai University on Osaka. She has worked as a lawyer, civil servant, IT consultant, and university teacher and has also lived in Cambridge, UK and Washington, DC. She has published 6 books of poetry, one of which (*Drag down to unlock or place an emergency call*, Pitt Street Poetry, 2013) won the 2014 Australian Prime Minister's Literary Award. Her work has been translated into multiple languages including Italian and Indonesian. She lives in Canberra and is a former poetry editor of *The Canberra Times*.

Shane Strange was born in Melbourne and grew up in Queensland. He has worked in bookselling and in banking (including for a Japanese bank). He is currently lives in Canberra and works at the University of Canberra, where he is a doctoral candidate in creative writing. As well as writing poetry and prose, he is publisher at Recent Work Press, a small press based in Canberra.

Ellen van Neerven is an Indigenous Australian writer belonging to the Yugambeh people of South East Queensland. She is the author of the poetry volume *Comfort Food* (UQP, 2016) and the fiction collection, *Heat and Light* (UQP, 2014) which won numerous awards.

初出一覧　Acknowledgments

For the Poems in English

'Three Kings to the City' was published under the title 'Bus' in Axon Capsule 1: Poetry on the Move 2015.

'The Weathercock' was first published in *Chromatic* (UWA Publishing, 2017).

'Asperger's Diagnosis: a Fugue' from *First… Then…: Poems from Planet Autism* (Ginninderra Press, 2012).

'Rain Dance I' from *Sangam House*, India, 2017, http://poetry.sangamhouse.org/2017/05/niloofar-fanaiyan/ and *Ley Lines and the Rustling of Cedar* (Recent Work Press, 2018).

'Love and Tradition' from *Comfort Food* (University of Queensland Press, 2016) .

'Contemplating the Gap' from *Goodbye, Cruel* (Pitt St Poetry, 2017).

'In Other Universes' from *Tract*, (Recent Work Press, 2017).

'Rubbish' from *Exhumed* (Grand Parade Poets, NSW, 2015).

'Fire' from *Sangam House* (India, 2017, http://poetry.sangamhouse.org/2017/05/niloofar-fanaiyan/).

'The Winchester Diver' was first published in *Quintet* (Staple First Editions, 1993) and in *Analogue/Digital* (Smith/Doorstop, 2015).

'Plumber', finalist in the 2018 international *Aesthetica* Creative Writing Competition (poetry), and published in the *Aesthetica Creative Writing Annual 2018,* York, UK: Aesthetica Publishing, 36; published in *Stride Magazine* (UK), November 2016, http://stridemagazine.blogspot.com.au; published in *Moonlight on Oleander: Prose Poems* (University of Western Australia Publishing, 2018).

For Translations in Japanese

The earlier versions of Japanese translations of 'Three Kings to the City', 'Join Roger on his Journey and Be Lulled to Sleep', 'Rubbish' and 'Watermelon' were published in *Hikone-ronsō* No. 416 (May 2018).

「山王発市街行」「おやすみロジャーといっしょに旅していっしょ寝よう」「ゴミ」「スイカ」(『彦根論叢』416号、2018年5月)

The publication of this anthology is supported by the Japanese government's KAKENHI research grant, 15KK0049.

We acknowledge the support of the Neilma Sidney Literary Travel Fund, The Myer Foundation and Writers Victoria in enabling Ellen Van Neerven and Melinda Smith to travel to Japan for this project.

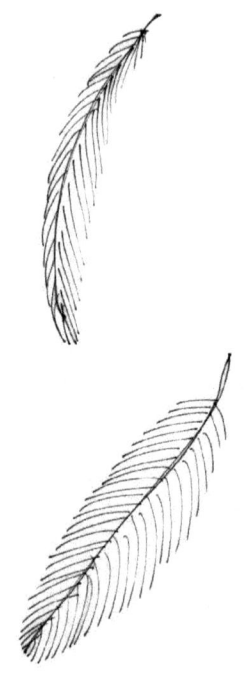

Lightning Source UK Ltd.
Milton Keynes UK
UKHW011240180522
403171UK00006B/501